BOTTOM EDGE OF COVER TAPED
— EVS 2/22

Black Hawk's War

Georgene Poulakidas

The Rosen Publishing Group's
PowerKids Press™
PRIMARY SOURCE

For Nicholas Petsas

Published in 2006 by The Rosen Publishing Group, Inc.
29 East 21st Street, New York, NY 10010

Copyright © 2006 by The Rosen Publishing Group, Inc.

First Edition

Editor: Eric Fein
Book Design: Erica Clendening
Photo Researcher: Amy Feinberg
Photo Credits: Cover, p. 14 Wisconsin Historical Society; p. 4 Private Collection/Bridgeman Art Library, (inset) Free Library, Philadelphia, PA, USA/Bridgeman Art Library: p. 6 Library of Congress Prints and Photographs Division, (inset bottom) National Archives; p. 6 (inset top), p. 8 (right) © Smithsonian American Art Museum, Washington, DC/ Art Resource, NY; p. 8 (left) Map & Geography Library, University of Illinois at Urbana – Champaign – Champaign; p. 10 Rudy L. Ruggles Collection, The Newberry Library, Chicago, (inset) State Historical Society of Iowa, Des Moines; p. 12 Northern Illinois University Libraries; p. 12 (inset), p. 14 (inset) Courtesy of the Illinois State Historical Library; p. 16 Minnesota Historical Society; p. 18 Library of Congress Geography and Map Division; p. 18 (inset), p. 20 (right) © Board of Trustees, National Gallery of Art, Washington; p. 20 (left) Rare Books Division, The New York Public Library, Astor, Lenox and Tilden Foundations.

Library of Congress Cataloging-in-Publication Data

Poulakidas, Georgene.
    Black Hawk's war / Georgene Poulakidas.
    p. cm. — (Primary sources of American wars)
    Includes bibliographical references and index.
    Contents: Troubles begin — Black Hawk opposes a treaty — Forced from their land — Black Hawk returns — The battle of Stillman's Run — The battle of Wisconsin Heights — The battle at Bad Axe — The end of the war — Black Hawk's final years.
    ISBN 1-4042-2682-6 (lib. bdg.)
    1. Black Hawk War, 1832—Juvenile literature. 2. Black Hawk, Sauk chief, 1767–1838—Juvenile literature. 3. Sauk Indians—Kings and rulers—Biography—Juvenile literature. [1. Black Hawk War, 1832. 2. Black Hawk, Sauk chief, 1767–1838. 3. Sauk Indians. 4. Indians of North America—Middle West.] I. Title. II. Series.

    E83.83.P68 2006
    973.5'6—dc22
                                                                    2003023808

Manufactured in the United States of America

Contents

Native Americans hunted buffalo only for food, clothing, and shelter. White settlers usually hunted buffalo for sport. In the 1800s, hunting by white settlers reduced the buffalo population from about 60 million to about 1,000.

Troubles Begin

America entered a time of great change and growth at the beginning of the nineteenth century. Thousands of white **settlers** from the East began to travel west across the country. They were searching for a better way of life. They wanted to set up new homes and businesses and to own land. However, the settlers were not moving to empty lands. Native American tribes, such as the Sauk and the Fox of the Midwest, had been living on these lands for many years.

Many settlers took over Native American lands. Settlers often killed buffalo, which Native Americans used for food, clothing, and shelter. This angered Native Americans. Fighting soon broke out between whites and Native Americans in many places across the country.

■ *Many families headed to the West to find a better way of life. The trip often took months. At night, settlers set up camps before continuing their trip in the morning.*

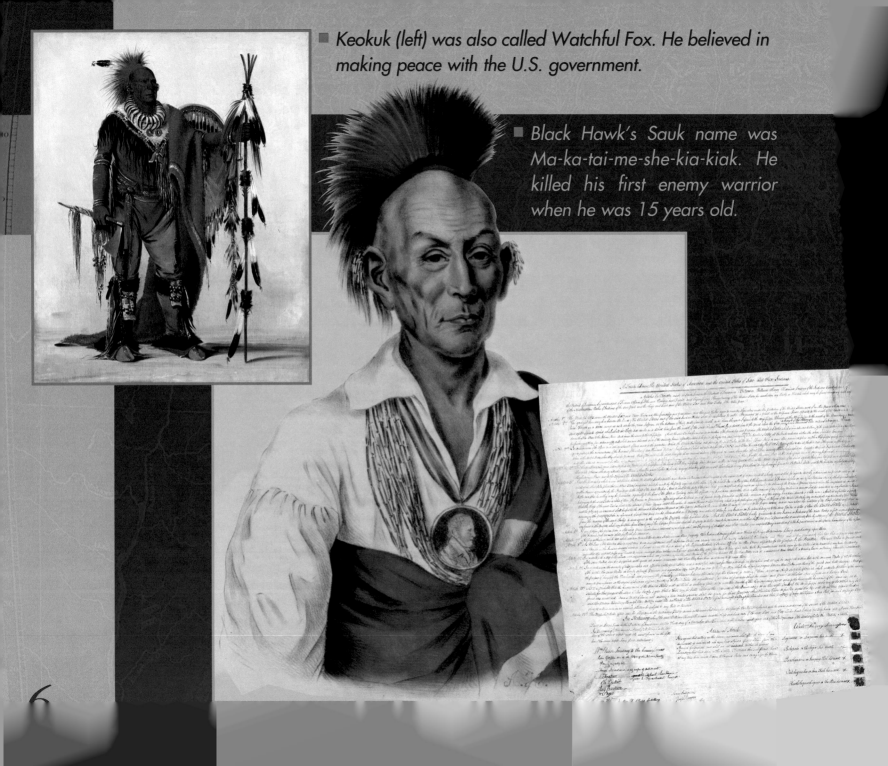

■ Keokuk (left) was also called Watchful Fox. He believed in making peace with the U.S. government.

■ Black Hawk's Sauk name was Ma-ka-tai-me-she-kia-kiak. He killed his first enemy warrior when he was 15 years old.

Black Hawk Opposes a Treaty

In 1804, the Sauk and Fox tribes signed a **treaty** with the U.S. government. The tribes agreed to give up their land in Illinois. In return, they received a yearly payment of about $1,000. Under this treaty, the tribes could continue to live on the land as long as the U.S. government owned it. However, the treaty stated that if the government sold the land, the tribes would have to move.

The Sauk war chief, Keokuk, agreed to obey the treaty and moved to Iowa. Black Hawk, another Sauk leader, refused to leave the land. Black Hawk opposed the treaty because he believed that the tribes had been tricked into signing it. Black Hawk and Keokuk became enemies over this disagreement.

■ *This 1804 treaty (left) required that the Sauk and the Fox give up about 50 million acres of land to the U.S. government.*

This is a map of Illinois from 1824. The left side of the green area at the top shows the territory used by the Sauk and Fox tribes.

Forced from Their Land

Black Hawk and his followers chose to stay at the Sauk village, Saukenuk, in Illinois. This village was located at the place where the Rock River and the Mississippi River meet.

Over the years, white settlers had taken over most of Saukenuk. Many settlers attacked Sauk women and children. Black Hawk complained to the U.S. government. However, nothing was done to stop the attacks.

In 1831, Black Hawk warned the settlers that he would fight them if they did not leave Saukenuk. The settlers contacted John Reynolds, the governor of Illinois. Reynolds ordered that Black Hawk and his people be removed. A state **militia**, accompanied by U.S. army troops, went to the village. Black Hawk and his followers were forced to move west, across the Mississippi River.

■ *Saukenuk was a good place for farming and fishing. This painting shows Sauk and Fox people in canoes.*

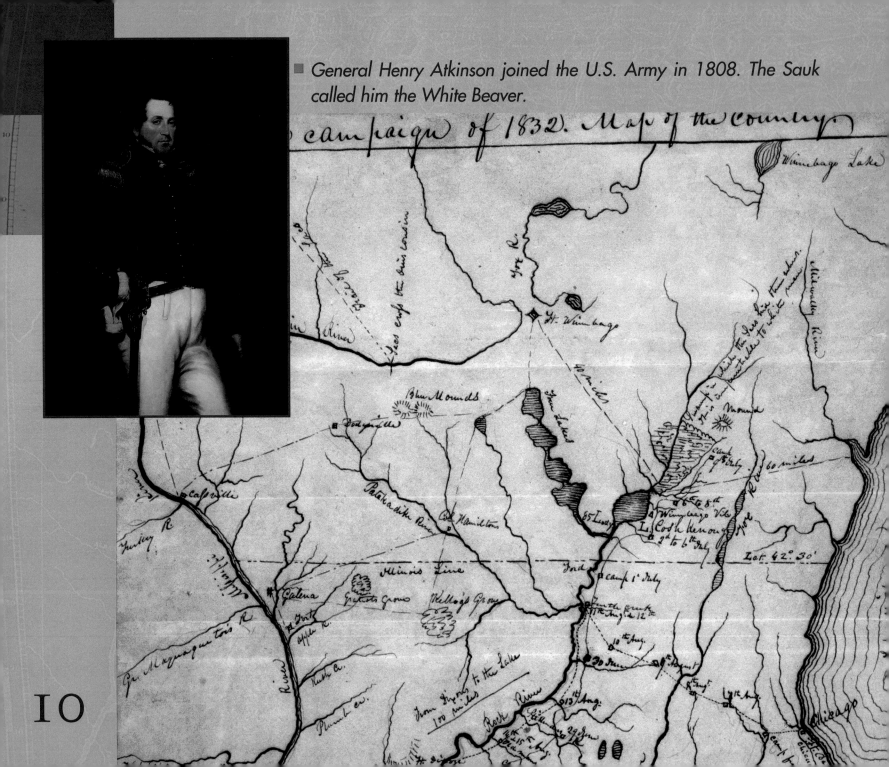

General Henry Atkinson joined the U.S. Army in 1808. The Sauk called him the White Beaver.

Black Hawk Returns

Black Hawk and his people suffered from hunger on their new, less fruitful land. On April 5, 1832, Black Hawk and his followers recrossed the Mississippi River and made their way along the Rock River. They were returning to Saukenuk for the spring crop planting. Black Hawk's followers consisted of about 500 men and 1,000 women, children, and old men.

When Governor Reynolds was notified about this, he once again called for the army to drive Black Hawk and his people out of Illinois. General Henry Atkinson was in charge of this campaign against Black Hawk. He sent **messengers** to Black Hawk, ordering that he and his followers leave the state. Black Hawk refused. On April 9, 1832, U.S. forces began their chase of Black Hawk. Black Hawk's War had begun.

■ *This map shows the areas of northern Illinois and southern Wisconsin where Black Hawk's War was fought. It also includes the paths and places used by both Black Hawk's people and the U.S. Army.*

It is believed that when Black Hawk and his men attacked Major Stillman's troops, Stillman (left) was one of the first to run away. For this reason, the soldiers began calling the battle, the Battle of Stillman's Run.

The Battle of Stillman's Run

On May 12, 1832, more soldiers joined the chase. Major Isaiah Stillman was one of the leaders of these troops. Stillman had about 300 soldiers with him. When Black Hawk heard of this, he sent a group of his followers to Stillman, carrying a white flag. This flag was a sign of **surrender**. However, some of Stillman's soldiers thought it was a trick and attacked Black Hawk's people. Several other Native Americans returned to Black Hawk and told him about the attack.

On May 14, Black Hawk attacked the army camp with about 45 warriors. Stillman and his men were surprised by the sudden appearance and fighting spirit of Black Hawk's warriors. The soldiers ran away.

■ *The Battle of Stillman's Run (left) is also known as the Battle of Sycamore Creek. This is because the fighting took place at the point where Sycamore Creek flowed into the Rock River.*

After his success during Black Hawk's War, Henry Dodge (left) served in the U.S. Congress. He first served in the House of Representatives and later in the Senate.

The Battle of Wisconsin Heights

Black Hawk and his people then went north to the area of Lake Koshkonong near the **headwaters** of Rock River in Michigan territory. Today, this **territory** is the state of Wisconsin. For many weeks this was Black Hawk's home. However, Black Hawk soon learned that army forces led by Henry Dodge and Alexander Henry were closing in. Black Hawk tried to move his people to safety. They headed toward the Wisconsin River. On July 21, 1832, Dodge and Henry's troops caught up with Black Hawk's group as they prepared to cross the river. Some of the Sauk were able to escape the fighting by floating down the Wisconsin River toward Iowa. Others battled the U.S. troops until nightfall. During the Battle of Wisconsin Heights, many women and children escaped down the river.

■ *This painting shows the area where the Battle of Wisconsin Heights was fought.*

16

The Battle of Bad Axe

Black Hawk decided to lead his people to the safety of the Sauk land in Iowa. On August 1, 1832, his group reached the Mississippi River. However, they found themselves trapped on the river's eastern shore, near Bad Axe, Wisconsin. U.S. troops had been able to follow the Sauks' trail, which included the bodies of those who had died from hunger or battle **injuries**.

Some Sauk were able to make it to the other side of the Mississippi River. Others drowned in its powerful waters. Soon, the American steamship *Warrior* approached the Sauk as they were crossing the river. Black Hawk did not think his people would be in danger because he knew the ship's captain. Black Hawk put a white cloth on a pole as an offer of peace. However, U.S. soldiers on the *Warrior* opened fire on the Indians.

■ *This painting shows the Battle of Bad Axe. Many of the Native Americans killed at this battle were women and children who were trying to cross the Mississippi River to safety.*

This painting shows Black Hawk (third from left) with five other Sauk prisoners.

18

The End of the War

By the next day, the Battle of Bad Axe was over. Black Hawk's War had ended. Black Hawk managed to escape, but he was captured on August 27, 1832. The cost in life for the Sauk was high. Of the original 1,500 people who followed Black Hawk, only about 150 survived this bloody war. The remaining Sauk settled in Iowa, near the Des Moines River.

This loss of the war pushed other midwestern tribes, such as the Potawatomi, to give up their land. In 1833, the last treaty concerning the Native American Indians of Illinois was arranged. The remaining tribes gave up all of their land in northeastern Illinois. After the war, Black Hawk spent many months in prison. He was first held in Jefferson Barracks, Missouri. He was later moved to Fortress Monroe in Virginia.

■ *This picture shows Fortress Monroe in Virginia, the largest stone fort ever built in America.*

LIFE
OF
MA-KA-TAI-ME-SHE-KIA-KIAK
OR
BLACK HAWK,

EMBRACING THE

TRADITION OF HIS NATION—INDIAN WARS IN WHICH HE HAS
BEEN ENGAGED—CAUSE OF JOINING THE BRITISH IN THEIR
LATE WAR WITH AMERICA, AND ITS HISTORY—DES-
CRIPTION OF THE ROCK-RIVER VILLAGE—MAN-
NERS AND CUSTOMS—ENCROACHMENTS BY
THE WHITES, CONTRARY TO TREATY—
REMOVAL FROM HIS VILLAGE IN 1831.

WITH AN ACCOUNT OF THE CAUSE

AND

GENERAL HISTORY

OF THE

LATE WAR,

HIS SURRENDER AND CONFINEMENT AT
JEFFERSON BARRACKS,

AND

TRAVELS THROUGH THE UNITED STATES.

DICTATED BY HIMSELF.

CINCINNATI:
1833.

WILBERFORCE EAMES
INDIAN COLLECTION

This is the title page of the book that Black Hawk wrote about his life. The book was published in 1833.

Black Hawk's Final Years

While still a prisoner, Black Hawk met President Andrew Jackson at the White House and was sent on a tour of eastern U.S. cities. After the tour, Black Hawk was returned to Fortress Monroe. He was released into the custody of his Sauk enemy, Keokuk. The U.S. government had made Keokuk Black Hawk's **guardian**. Black Hawk was angered by this. He returned with Keokuk to the Sauk land in Iowa. Black Hawk later told his life story to a U.S. government official. His story was **published** in 1833. Black Hawk died in Iowa in 1838.

Fighting between Native Americans and the U.S. government would continue for another 50 years. Black Hawk's War is remembered as an important part of the early battles.

■ *Black Hawk died on October 3, 1838. This painting shows his burial.*

Timeline

1804	Sauk and Fox tribes sign treaty with the United States.
1831	Illinois governor John Reynolds orders the state militia to remove Black Hawk and his people from their land.
April 1832	Black Hawk's War begins after Black Hawk and his people cross the Mississippi River back into Illinois.
May 14, 1832	The Battle of Stillman's Run is fought.
July 1832	The Battle of Wisconsin Heights is fought.
August 1, 1832	The Battle of Bad Axe is fought. Black Hawk escapes.
August 2, 1832	Black Hawk's War ends.
August 27, 1832	Black Hawk is captured.
1833	Final treaty is signed between the Indians of Illinois and the United States.
1833	Black Hawk meets President Andrew Jackson and tours eastern U.S. cities.
July 1838	Black Hawk dies in Iowa.

Glossary

guardian (GAR-dee-uhn) Someone who has the legal responsibility to look after someone else.

headwaters (HED-waw-turz) The source of a stream or river.

injuries (IN-jur-eez) Damage or harm done to a person.

messengers (MESS-uhn-jurz) People who carry messages.

militia (muh-LISH-uh) A group of citizens trained to fight but who only serve in time of emergency.

published (PUHB-lisht) To have produced and distributed a book, magazine, newspaper, or any other printed material so that people can buy it.

settlers (SET-lerz) People who make a home in a new place.

surrender (suh-REN-dur) To give up, or to admit that you are beaten, in a fight or battle.

territory (TER-uh-tor-ee) The land and waters under the control of a state, nation, or ruler.

treaty (TREE-tee) A formal agreement between two or more groups of people.

Index

Primary Sources

Cover: *The Battle of Bad Axe August 2, 1832* [c. 1940s]. Painting by Cal Peters. Villa Louis Historic Site in Prairie du Chien. **Page 4 (inset):** *Hunting the Buffalo* [c. nineteenth century]. Lithograph. Artist unknown. Free Library, Philadelphia, Pennsylvania. **Page 4:** *Advice on the Prairie* [c. nineteenth century]. Oil on canvas by William Tylee Ranney. Private collection. **Page 6 (inset, top):** *Keokuk (The Watchful Fox), Chief of the Tribe* [1835]. George Catlin. Smithsonian American Art Museum. **Page 6 (inset, below):** Ratified Indian Treaty #43: Sauk & Foxes Nov. 3, 1804 [1804]. National Archives. **Page 6:** *Ma-Ka-Tai-Me-She-Kia-Kiah, or Black Hawk, a Saukie brave* [c. 1838]. Lithograph published by F. W. Greenough from *History of the Indian Tribes of North America* by McKenney and Hall. Library of Congress. **Page 8 (inset):** *Illinois* [1824]. Young and Delleker. Map & Geography Library, University of Illinois at Urbana-Champaign. **Page 8:** *Sauk and Fox Sailing in Canoes* [1837–1839]. Oil on canvas by George Catlin. Smithsonian American Art Museum. **Page 10 (inset):** Henry Atkinson [c. 1824]. Oil on canvas by George Catlin. State Historical Society of Iowa. **Page 10:** Black Hawk War (Map of Indian war of 1832 made by one who was there, Col. Edwin Rose) [1832]. Pen-and-ink. Rudy Lamont Ruggles Collection/Newberry Library. **Page 12 (inset):** Major Isaiah Stillman [Date unknown]. Illinois State Historical Library. **Page 12:** *The Battle of Sycamore Creek* [Date unknown]. Artist unknown. Northern Illinois University Libraries. **Page 14 (inset):** Henry Dodge [Date unknown]. Illinois State Historical Library. **Page 14:** *Wisconsin Heights Battlefield* [1856]. Painting. by S. M. Brookes. Wisconsin Historical Society. **Page 16:** *Massacre at Bad Axe* [c. 1848]. Henry Lewis from *The Valley of the Mississippi, Illustrated.* Minnesota Historical Society. **Page 18 (inset):** *Black Hawk and Five Other Saukie Prisoners* [c. 1860s]. Oil on card mounted on paperboard by George Catlin. National Gallery of Art. **Page 18:** Fortress Monroe, Va. and its vicinity [c. 1862]. Jacob Wells. Library of Congress. **Page 20 (inset):** *Life of Black Hawk* title page [1833]. First edition. Rare Books Division/ New York Public Library. **Page 20:** *Funeral of Black Hawk-Saukie* [c. 1860s]. Oil on card mounted on paperboard by George Catlin. National Gallery of Art.

Web Sites

Due to the changing nature of Internet links, PowerKids Press has developed an online list of Web sites related to the topic of this book. This site is updated regularly. Please use this link to access the list:
http://www.powerkidslinks.com/psaw/bhw/